The Last Days of Steam in Gloucestershire

Leaving Gloucester on the Midland Railway route, a Nottingham–Bristol express hauled by L.M.S. Jubilee class 4-6-0 No 45579 "Punjab" climbs away from Eastgate Station between California and Farm Street Crossings on 24.12.62.

The Last Days of Steam in Gloucestershire

Ben Ashworth

ALAN SUTTON

1986

Alan Sutton Publishing Limited
30 Brunswick Road
Gloucester GL1 1JJ

First published 1983
Reprinted 1984
Reprinted 1986

British Library Cataloguing in Publication Data

Ashworth, Ben
    Last days of steam in Gloucestershire.
    1. Locomotives—England—Gloucestershire
    I. Title
    625.2′61′094241   TJ603.4.G7

ISBN 0 86299 057 2

Typesetting and origination by
Alan Sutton Publishing Limited
Printed in Great Britain

Preface

Something akin to a revolution occurred on the railways during the period of seven or eight years which these photographs illustrate.

In addition to the coming of diesel power, branch lines rapidly disappeared and, of the 90 or so Gloucestershire (old style) stations and halts open in 1959 only about a dozen remained by 1966 when steam power had finally been banished from the Western Region of British Rail.

The Gloucester–Cheltenham area was not lacking in the quantity or diversity of its rail traffic and with the traditions of two big railway companies firmly established, there were some interesting comparisons of motive power and operating practices where they ran side by side between Cheltenham and Standish.

At Cheltenham Lansdown there were also the regular and somewhat incongruous appearances of trains from the Southern

Region on the through trains from Southampton, although by the end of the 1950's only one such train remained in each direction, using the G.W.R.'s Cheltenham terminus at St. James instead of Lansdown. With the occasional L.N.E.R. loco working through from the Midlands it was possible to see engines of all four major companies passing Lansdown Junction, until the Southampton service was finally withdrawn in September 1961.

Even though the line between Cheltenham Lansdown and Gloucester was quadrupled during the 1939–45 war, this section would often be full to capacity, especially on Saturdays in Summer. At the Gloucester end, traffic from South Wales merged with that feeding in from the former Somerset & Dorset Joint via Bath and Mangotsfield and from South West England using both G.W. and L.M.S. routes converging at Yate. Similarly at Cheltenham, G.W. and L.M.S. routes from Birmingham came together at Lansdown Junction. Gloucester itself had the added problem of South Wales – Swindon traffic conflicting with the north–south flow at Tramway and Gloucester South Junctions, but once the S. & D.J.R. route to Bournemouth had closed and the motorways begun to take over much of the holiday traffic there was no longer such congestion and in 1967, with the help of automatic signalling, the Gloucester–Cheltenham line reverted once more to double track. At the time of writing about half (roughly 130 miles) the mileage of the original Gloucestershire rail system remains. Doubtless what is left works more efficiently, but what it has gained in this respect has been lost tenfold in interest and character.

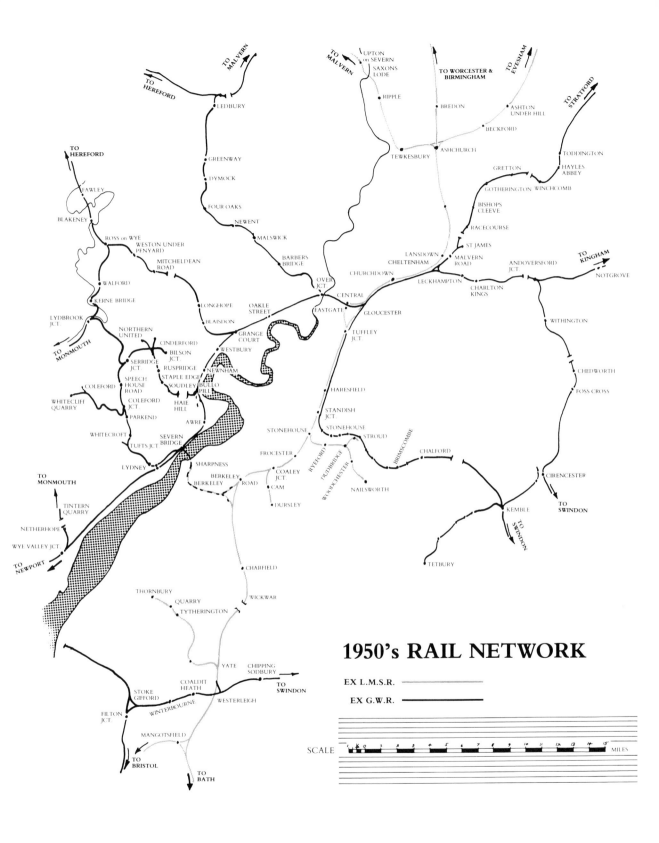

1950's RAIL NETWORK

EX L.M.S.R. ....
EX G.W.R. ————

SCALE ————————————————— MILES

A typical weekday scene at Gloucester looking from the covered way connecting Eastgate (L.M.S.) and Central (G.W.) stations. Horton Road (G.W.) loco' shed is in the background and on the left G.W. "Castle" class 4–6–0 No 5017 "The Gloucestershire Regiment 28th 61st" is waiting to back on to the midday Paddington train, after its arrival from Cheltenham. A B.R. class 4 4–6–0 is at the turntable on the site of the original M.R. engine shed. The empty stock of a Bristol–Gloucester stopping train is being shunted and on the extreme right the 'down' "Cornishman" is entering Eastgate station. Date 2.12.61.

Interior of covered way connecting Eastgate and Central stations.

The midday departure for Paddington leaving Gloucester Central headed by G.W. "Castle" class 4-6-0 No 5017 "The Gloucestershire Regiment 28th 61st". Date 2.12.61.

G.W. 4-6-0's 5001 "Llandovery Castle" and 5008 "Raglan Castle" at Gloucester Central on 10.11.61.

'Up' and 'down' line scissors crossovers at Gloucester Central on 14.12.63. B.R. class 9 2-10-0 No 92236 heads west on a through freight, while a G.W. "Grange" and a diesel mechanical shunter make for Horton Road shed.

A pair of G.W. 2-8-2T's Nos 7221 and 7252 at Horton Road shed on 14.9.64; as seen from the Chalford 'railcar'.

A pair of G.W. 2-6-0's in Horton Road shed yard on 8.4.63. The 73xx class loco' on the turntable is a later version with modified cab.

The last evening of service for the Chalford 'railcar', on 31.10.64. G.W. 0-4-2T No 1458 takes water at Gloucester Central before leaving with the 9.28 p.m. depature, which was extended to Kemble on Saturdays.

G.W. 0-4-2T No 1472 propels an evening auto-train from Chalford past Tuffley Junction, Gloucester on 6.4.64. The junction for the Hempstead branch is in the foreground.

Hoar frost coats the Haresfield 'down' platform at 10.25 a.m. on 24.10.64 as L.M.S. class 5 4-6-0 44965 arrives with a Bristol–Gloucester stopping train. The wooden platform backed on to the G.W. lines which ran parallel with the L.M.S.R. between Tuffley and Standish Junctions. This section has since been reduced to two tracks with up and down loops commencing near the former road crossing.

Auto-trains meeting at Cashes Green Halt make a busy scene on Saturday 29.4.62. G.W. 0-4-2T 1473 is on the 'up' line and 1409 sandwiched between its coaches is about to leave for Gloucester.

Looking south towards Stonehouse from the road bridge at Standish on 8.8.64. G.W. 0-6-0PT No 3737 on a local from Chalford has been given priority over a West of England–Wolverhampton train which is waiting to cross on to the G.W. line.

Following on from the previous picture:– G.W. 4-6-0 No 5026 "Criccieth Castle" has just crossed from L.M.S. to G.W. lines with a West of England–Wolverhampton train and will continue past Gloucester on the avoiding line. G.W. 0-4-2T No 1472 is on the Gloucester–Chalford service and in the distance a G.W. "Hall" waits in one of the loops. Two months after this photograph was taken a new junction was installed just to the north of the road bridge, allowing London trains direct access to Gloucester Eastgate station. In 1968 after removal of the old Standish Junction the ex-G.W. track was lifted between Standish and Tuffley leaving only two tracks for all traffic.

On 20.7.61 half a mile south of Standish Junction, G.W. "Castle" class 4-6-0 No 5071 "Spitfire" brings the "Cheltenham Spa Express" around the two miles of continuous curve leading out of the Stroud Valley. Within three years of this date "Spitfire" was reduced to scrap metal at Sharpness.

Following on the heels of the "Cheltenham Spa Express", G.W. 0-4-2T No 1472 has been saddled with an additional load on the Chalford–Gloucester 'railcar'. With no station at Haresfield the G.W.R. had a clear run of 8¾ miles between Stonehouse Burdett Road and Gloucester, allowing speeds of 70 m.p.h. to be reached by these auto-trains.

On 11.4.61 a school's special returning from Swindon to Leicester traverses the Stroud Valley between Brimscombe Bridge and Ham Mill Halts. L.M.S. "Royal Scot" class 4-6-0 No 46112 "Sherwood Forester" provided the most unusual motive power for this special.

In a flurry of steam G.W. 2-6-2T's Nos 5184 and 6137 arrive back at Brimscombe after giving banking assistance up to Sapperton Sidings. G.W. 2-8-0 No 3850 is about to pull forward on to the main line in readiness for the climb. Date 22.1.63.

At Brimscombe station G.W. 2-8-0 No 2874 draws its train forward, with G.W. 2-6-2T No 4116 waiting to give assistance on the five mile climb. Date 22.2.62.

G.W. 0-4-2T No 1473 propels its Gloucester bound auto-train into Brimscombe station on 29.4.62. One of the banking loco's can be seen outside the shed.

A short distance up the line from Brimscombe, at the point where the Thames–Severn canal passed beneath, was St. Mary's Crossing Halt. In this picture, taken on 5.6.62, G.W. 4-6-0 No 7035 "Ogmore Castle" on the midday Cheltenham–Paddington takes a run at Chalford Bank.

Shortly before the withdrawal of the Gloucester–Chalford auto-train service, several types of steam and diesel loco's appeared briefly in place of the usual 0–4–2T. On 14.9.64, G.W. 2–6–2T No 4564 is seen pulling away from St. Mary's Crossing Halt. Having no auto-train apparatus, it is not permitted to propel the trailer in the normal way.

Chalford station on 13.2.60. G.W. 0–4–2T No 1433 waits in the station yard before returning to Gloucester.

An early morning Cheltenham–Paddington train headed by a G.W. 2–6–2T and "Castle" make a vigorous attack on the 1 in 57/75 incline at Chalford. Date 3.8.61.

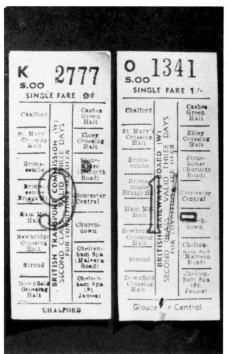

Tickets issued on the Chalford "railcar".

The Minister of Transport has given his
consent to the Board's proposal to
discontinue all passenger train services
from the following stations and halts
on the SWINDON—GLOUCESTER (Central)
section of line:-

PURTON   BRIMSCOMBE BRIDGE HALT
MINETY & ASHTON KEYNES   HAM MILL HALT
OAKSEY HALT   BOWBRIDGE CROSSING HALT
CHALFORD   DOWNFIELD CROSSING HALT
ST. MARY'S CROSSING HALT   CASHES GREEN HALT
BRIMSCOMBE   EBLEY CROSSING HALT

The terms of the Minister's consent can
be inspected at local booking offices

The services will be withdrawn
on and from Monday, 2nd November, 1964

Closure Notice.

On 3.8.61 at Chalford. Austerity 2-8-0 No 90676 eases its load down towards Brimscombe.

From the same view point on 2.8.62 . G.W. 2-8-2T No 7236 with an 'up' freight, negotiates the steep wooded slope facing Chalford village.

Retaining arches are needed to support the railway on the steep slope facing Chalford. The train is the midday Cheltenham–Paddington, headed by G.W. 4-6-0 No 7035 "Ogmore Castle". Date 25.7.62.

G.W. 4-6-0 No 6923 "Croxteth Hall" rolls down hill past Frampton Mansell with a train of sand on 30.5.62. Frampton Crossing signal box is just visible where the line disappears and below this point is evidence of an earlier form of transport in the remains of Puck's Mill Lock on the Thames–Severn canal.

There's no shortage of condensed steam as G.W. 2-8-0 No 3853 slogs up to Sapperton Tunnel with a coal train on a very cold day in January 1963. . . .

. . . and disappears into the snow encrusted tunnel entrance with G.W. 2-6-2T No 4100 bringing up the rear.

The short break in the tunnel at the top of Sapperton Bank on 30.4.60 with G.W. 4-6-0 No 5924 "Dinton Hall" heading a London bound special.

Cirencester Town station yard shortly before its closure in 1965. In the centre background is the tall station building, originally the terminus of the main line from Swindon.

On 28.2.61 G.W. 0-6-0 No 2250 struggles up the eastern slope of the Cotswolds with the daily Swindon–Gloucester pick-up goods. The location is Hailes Wood between Coates and Sapperton.

Steam hangs low in the hazy sunshine on a very cold morning early in March 1962. The G.W. 2-6-2T is heading a Cheltenham St. James–Kingham train up the Chelt Valley past Charlton Kings reservoir.

On 2.8.61 an evening Cheltenham St. James–Kingham train climbs towards Sandywell Park Tunnel and Andoversford Junction.

The Andoversford Junction signalman waits with the single line token as S.R. class 'U' 2-6-0 No 31791 pulls away from the station with the last regular Cheltenham–Southampton train on 9.9.61.

Interior of Andoversford Junction signal box showing block instruments.

On 11.7.64 at Andoversford, B.R. class 2 2-6-0 No 78001 has just arrived from Cheltenham to collect another load of lifted track. The contractor's cranes and diesel loco. are at work on the remaining section of the Kingham line and to the right is the bare trackbed of the M. & S.W.J.R. Much of the embankment has since been removed to make way for the A40 Andoversford by-pass.

General view of Withington station on 19.7.63 during track removal operations. The contractors diesel is coming through the station with a load of track lifted from near Chedworth.

G.W. 2-8-0 No 2872 has a clearance problem at Withington during recovery of track from the M. & S.W.J.R. on 19.7.63.

S.R. class 'U' 2-6-0 No 31803 climbs out of the Colne Valley on 10.2.61 with the afternoon Cheltenham–Southampton. The train is passing the site of Chedworth Woods timber sidings, a mile and a half from Withington station.

On 7.7.61 S.R. class 'U' 2-6-0 No 31629 climbs through Chedworth Wood with the 1.52 p.m. Cheltenham St. James–Southampton. The Gloucestershire Nature Conservancy Trust now has a reserve here.

On 14.5.60 the Gloucestershire Railway Society ran a special to Southampton headed by G.W. 4-4-0 No 3440 "City of Truro"; here it is on the outward journey passing through Chedworth Wood.

A cold wet day at the end of June 1963. G.W. 2-6-0 No 6344 struggles towards the wooden station at Chedworth with a load of sleepers recovered from Fosse Cross.

The bleak Cotswold top on 18.2.60 with a G.W. 9400 class 0–6–0PT climbing towards the summit at Notgrove with a pick-up goods bound for Kingham.

High summer on the Cotswolds. An evening train from Cheltenham near the end of the climb to Notgrove headed by G.W. 2-6-2T No 4106. Date 2.7.62.

Gloucestershire's highest railway station as seen from the B4068 road bridge at a little short of 800 ft. G.W. 2-6-0 No 7319 is at work with a demolition train in Notgrove station on 8.5.64.

The 'up' "Cheltenham Spa Express" makes an explosive start from Cheltenham Malvern Road on 8.5.64. G.W. 2-6-2T No 4564 is about to make the short sprint to Gloucester Central, where the train will reverse and continue diesel hauled to Paddington.

Having taken water, G.W. 2-8-0 No 3816 and B.R. class 9 2-10-0 No 92000 leave Cheltenham for the Honeybourne line via Malvern Road East Junction. The rear end of G.W. 2-6-2T No 4141 protrudes from Malvern Road shed.

With Great Western Road in the foreground, the 'down' "Cornishman" headed by G.W. "Castle" class 4-6-0 No 7001 "Sir James Milne" approaches Cheltenham Malvern Road East Junction. This was the last 'down' "Cornishman" to use the G.W. route from Birmingham and also the last to be steam hauled. From 10.9.62 the "Cornishman" was diesel hauled on the L.M.S. route, via (but not stopping at!) Lansdown station. The photograph was taken from a wall overlooking St. James Station yard.

From the same viewpoint as the previous picture, on 7.5.64. G.W. 2-6-2T No 4564 leaves Cheltenham St. James with the 2.35 p.m. to Swindon via Gloucester Central.

One of the many northbound expresses on a summer Saturday rolls into Cheltenham Lansdown on 18.7.64 behind a grimy L.M.S. "Jubilee" class 4-6-0 No 45602 "British Honduras".

Cheltenham Malvern Road East, where the short branch from St James Station made a junction with the Honeybourne line. L.M.S. class 5 4-6-0 45006 has just left Malvern Road with the S.O. 11.22 a.m. from Newquay and is about to veer to its left for Birmingham. The G.W. route to Birmingham was nearly 9 miles longer than that of the L.M.S. and was not completed until 1906. The track was finally lifted in 1979 after several years with little or no traffic.

The G.W. and L.M.S. routes from Birmingham converged at Lansdown Junction, Cheltenham. In this scene L.M.S. class 4F 0-6-0's, Nos 43940 and 44394 return north running light and L.M.S. "Jubilee" class 4-6-0 No 45565 "Victoria" is about to leave Lansdown station with the Nottingham–Bristol on 24.5.62.

G.W. "Castle" class 4-6-0 No 5054 "Earl of Ducie", heads south from Huntingbutts Tunnel on the northern outskirts of Cheltenham with a West of England train on 29.8.64.

L.M.S. "Jubilee" class 4–6–0 45565 "Victoria" makes an impressively rapid getaway from Cheltenham Lansdown with the 7.35 a.m. Nottingham–Bristol on 24.5.62.

Cheltenham Racecourse station and a southbound train in July 1966.

On 18.7.64 the Bishops Cleeve platforms have been removed but the unusual stone-built signal box still remains. G.W. 4-6-0 No. 7023 "Penrice Castle" seems to have fire problems as it heads north with a summer Saturday extra. The L.M.S.R. also had a station for Cleeve some 2 miles to the west.

Brush class 4 No D1600 approaching Gotherington station on 23.7.66. At this point the railway passed between Dixton (in background) and Nottingham Hills before swinging south to Cheltenham.

A train service of sorts still survived between Stratford on Avon and Gloucester in 1966, although all the intermediate stations and halts closed when the 0–4–2T operated service between Honeybourne and Cheltenham St. James ceased in 1960. On 3.9.66 a Gloucester R.C. & W. Co single unit is seen, southbound, at the southern entrance to Greet tunnel, forming the 15.45 from Leamington Spa. This service ran 36 miles non-stop between Stratford-on-Avon and Gloucester.

In the last year of steam operated West of England trains over the G.W. route from Birmingham, G.W. 4-6-0 No 7912 "Little Linford Hall" heads northwestwards into Greet tunnel, near Winchcombe, having done a near 'U' turn, following the foot of the Cotswold escarpment. Date 3.7.65.

B.R. "Britannia" Pacific No 70045 "Lord Rowallan" takes the 8.0 a.m. Wolverhampton–Ilfracombe round the long curve past the site of Winchcombe station. Date 3.7.65.

On 13.6.59, two years before the passenger service ceased, M.R. class 3F 0-6-0 43520 is about to leave Tewkesbury with an evening train for Upton on Severn.

The picturesque station at Ripple on 5.7.60. L.M.S. class 3F 0-6-0T No 47506 of Barnwood shed Gloucester is approaching with the 5.10 p.m. Ashchurch–Upton on Severn.

A short distance from Ripple station the Ashchurch–Great Malvern branch crossed the River Severn at Saxon's Lode. In this copy of a Kodachrome transparency, the early morning train from Upon on Severn is seen crossing the bridge hauled by M.R. class 3F 0-6-0 No 43520. Date 13.6.59.

In this scene, L.M.S. "Jubilee" class 4–6–0 No 45562 "Alberta" makes a detour (from the original M.R. route) via Worcester Shrub Hill and is about to pass Worcester Tunnel Junction with the 8.40 a.m. Bristol–Sheffield. The through freight line (since severed) diverges to the left and on the right a 52 van train from Hereford hauled by G.W. 4–6–0 No 6837 "Forthampton Grange" is waiting to follow on. Date 30.4.63.

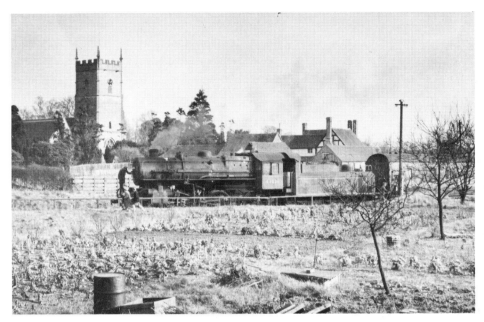

At Ashchurch on 19.3.62 L.M.S. class 4 2-6-0 No 43036 waits with the 4.30 p.m. to Redditch.

An evening Gloucester–Worcester–Birmingham stopping train passing Churchdown on 28.4.64 headed by L.M.S. "Jubilee" class 4-6-0 No 45653 "Barham".

A lone photographer stands at the end of Churchdown station platform, as a summer Saturday Wolverhampton–West of England train approaches, headed by G.W. 4-6-0 No 7023 "Penrice Castle". Date 29.8.64.

Unrebuilt L.M.S. "Patriot" class 4-6-0 No 45504 "Royal Signals" passing Churchdown with a Bristol–Birmingham fitted freight on 5.7.61.

Rebuilt L.M.S. "Patriot" class 4–6–0 No 45532 "Illustrious" passing Churchdown with a Worcester–Gloucester stopping train on 22.7.61.

Super-power for an 'up Midland stopper' on 16.6.61. Of some 40 trains a day stopping at Churchdown, only 5 remained from L.M.S. days on the Gloucester–Birmingham New Street service. In this scene, schoolboys gaze in admiration and wonder at the rare appearance of L.M.S. "Royal Scot" class 4–6–0 No 46118 "Royal Welch Fusilier" on the 4.38 p.m. stopping train to Birmingham.

Interior of Churchdown signal box shortly before closure. 'Up' and 'down' relief lines were laid in 1942 to cope with increased wartime traffic, but these were lifted in 1967 when the signal box was closed, after installation of automatic signalling.

Gloucester Barnwood shed yard in February 1963. G.W. "Castle" class 4-6-0 No 5049 "Earl of Plymouth" is under repair. L.M.S. class 8F 2-8-0 48010 in steam and L.M.S. 4F 0-6-0 No 44092 at the coaling stage.

The centre pair of driving wheels from G.W. "Castle" class "Earl of Plymouth" in Barnwood shed yard in February 1963.

A grim scene in Barnwood shed yard at the start of the 1962/1963 winter. Coal fires are kept alight in an attempt to prevent freezing of equipment.

M.R. class 2P 4-4-0's Nos Nos 40537 and 40540 at Barnwood on 24.12.61 – not a safe place to leave such a trophy as the headboard to "The Waverley"! These were two of the last three seven foot driving wheel Midland Railway 4-4-0's.

Cab fittings of M.R. class 3F 0-6-0 No 43754.

One of the L.M.S. class 2P 4-4-0's, No 40696, leaving Barnwood on its way to the breaker's yard behind L.M.S. class 2 2-6-2T No 41243. Both loco's were from Bath shed and 40696 in particular had put in much hard work on the S. & D.J.R. Date 17.5.62.

40696 cabside.

Gloucester Barnwood shed yard on 16.7.62.
From left to right: L.M.S. 3F 0-6-0T 47417, G.W. 0-6-2T 6610, B.R. class 5 4-6-0, L.M.S. 4-6-0 45392, L.M.S. 0-6-0 44165, B.R. 2-10-0 92220 "Evening Star", L.M.S. 4-6-0 44828. The shed was closed in May 1964.

Christmas Eve in the roundhouse. A very 'Midland' collection of 0-6-0's at Barnwood in 1961; though there seems to be some doubt about the shed code. 3F No 43754 still has an 85E plate, 3F No 47623 and 4F 44272 carry 85C, the former Hereford shed code and 3F No 43645 is apparently homeless!

Engine Shed Junction, Gloucester. 31.12.62.

L.M.S. class 4F 0-6-0 No 44123 passing 'T' sidings on its way to Gloucester South Junction on 7.1.63. 44123 is at present (1982) awaiting restoration on the Mid-Hants line.

The 'up' "Cornishman" passing Gloucester Barnwood shed behind "Castle" class 4-6-0 5089 "Westminster Abbey" on 20.7.62.

The 'down' "Cornishman" passing Barnwood shed behind G.W. "Castle" class 4-6-0 No 5089 "Westminster Abbey" on 18.7.62. In front of the coaling stage are B.R. "Britannia" class 4-6-2 No 70049 "Solway Firth" and B.R. class 9 2-10-0 No 92220 "Evening Star". Barnwood Sidings Ground Frame, on the left, is now at Norchard, the Dean Forest Preservation Centre.

A Saturday afternoon in summer just north of Tramway Junction, Gloucester. L.M.S. "Jubilee" class 4-6-0 No 45650 "Blake" accelerates away with the Penzance–Bradford on 21.7.62.

M.R. class OF 0-4-0T No 41537 leads the way across Llanthony Swing bridge, heading west for the G.W.R. Docks Branch Sidings. It has travelled via California Crossing, The High Orchard branch and a reversal at Victoria Dock. Date 10.11.61.

Looking north from just inside the Southgate Street entrance to Gloucester Docks on 9.4.62. M.R. class OF 0-4-0T No 41535 awaits the removal of cars from the running line before proceeding to the Commercial Road entrance.

M.R. class OF 0-4-0T No 41537 crossing Park Road near California Crossing on its way to work in Gloucester Docks on the morning of 5.10.59.

An afternoon trip to the High Orchard Branch at California Crossing, with the main line crossing gates visible to the right of the signal box. The most unusual motive power is S. & D.J.R. class 7F 2-8-0 No 53806, which had developed a 'hot (axle) box' while returning to Bath after major overhaul at Derby. Date 12.5.61. Note the British Rail recruiting poster – this was shortly before Dr. Beeching became chairman of the British Railways Board!

California Crossing on 4.6.62 and the 'down' "Cornishman" headed by G.W. 4-6-0 No 5022 "Tenby Castle". This former Midland Railway route between Eastgate Station and Tuffley Junction was closed at the end of 1975.

On 27.11.65 the W.R. of B.R. ran a "Farewell to Steam" special from Paddington to Cheltenham and back. G.W. 4-6-0 No 7029 "Clun Castle" worked the train over part of the route and is seen here entering Gloucester Eastgate station from the south.

L.M.S. class 3F 0-6-0T No 47308 waiting at Barton Street Junction on 4.6.62 prior to working a local trip to Quedgeley.

Gloucester Eastgate carriage sidings on 27.5.61 with M.R. class 4P compound 4-4-0 No 1000 marshalling the stock for a Gloucestershire Railway Society special.

In 1980, from a similar viewpoint to that on p.69, only the platforms remain on the Eastgate station site.

The north end of Gloucester Eastgate station on 5.10.65 with L.M.S. class 4F 0–6–0 No 44269 passing on a local goods. In the background is the covered way leading to the Central station.

A once familiar sight near Hempstead on weekday mornings, looking from the main Bristol road towards Tuffley Junction. At one time the line crossed the canal and continued to Llanthony. Date 18.9.65.

Near its junction with the Hempstead branch, L.M.S. class 4F 0-6-0 No 44264 pushes its train of coal down the line to Bristol Road gasworks. Date 18.9.65.

The Stroud and Nailsworth branch on 14.5.65 with B.R. class 2 2-6-0 No 78004 returning to Stonehouse over the Stroudwater Canal near Ryeford. Judging by the bundle of sticks on the tender someone has recently planted their runner beans!

At Woodchester on 14.5.65 the platform is still intact but the brick foundations are being salvaged after the removal of the wooden station building. B.R. class 2 2-6-0 No 78004 is about to cross the Dursley road and continue on its way to Nailsworth.

The split level approaches to Nailsworth station and goods yard on 7.5.62. Standing at the water tank

The station building (since demolished) at Dudbridge on 23.8.65. The passenger service was withdrawn in 1947, but before World War 2 when the service was operated by M.R. 0-4-4T's, passengers changed here for Stroud Cheapside as it was then known.

is L.M.S. class 4F 0-6-0 No 44045.

On 7.7.63 the Gloucestershire Railway Society ran a special up the M.R. branch from Stonehouse; it is seen here approaching Stroud Wallgate station with L.M.S. class 3F 0-6-0T No 47308 in charge.

On 3.5.65 traffic is reduced to one wagon of coal as B.R. class 2 2-6-0 No 78001 leaves Dudbridge Junction for Stroud Wallgate. The Nailsworth branch is visible behind.

The goods yard at Stroud Wallgate on 7.5.62 with L.M.S. class 4F 0-6-0 No 44045 shunting. A bridge carrying the Swindon–Gloucester line is visible over the van roofs.

Steam loco's passing through, en route for the breakers' yards in South Wales were a familiar sight in the Gloucester area in the mid 1960's. Here, a long train comprised of a Standard '5' 4-6-0 and three "Merchant Navy" 4-6-2's was caught passing Frocester on 4.1.67. In the foreground is 35028 "Clan Line", since restored for main line running.

On 31.8.62 a few days before the withdrawal of the passenger service, the 09.55 from Dursley runs into Cam station – dead on time – according to the cloth mill clock. The loco' is L.M.S. class 2 2-6-0 No 46526.

B.R. class 2 2-6-0 No 78001 shunts the yard at Dursley on 6.3.65. This was one of the branch lines to survive into the diesel era.

The Sharpness branch engine crew at Berkeley Road in 1964.

A lamp on the Severn & Wye side of Berkeley Road station.

A trespass notice at Berkeley station. The Severn & Wye Railway was taken over jointly, by the G.W.R. and M.R. in 1894.

At Berkeley Road on 20.7.64. G.W. 4-6-0 No 6942 "Eshton Hall" heads an 'up' freight. Hymek No 7077 has recently arrived from the south and deposited its load of scrap metal bound for Sharpness docks. Condemned G.W. 2-8-0's Nos 4702, 2842 and 2852 will continue down to Sharpness behind the branch passenger loco.

G.W. 0–4–2T No 1445 propels the 08.15 departure for Sharpness away from Berkeley Road on 20.7.64.

The Gloucester breakdown train with L.M.S. class 4F No 44123 in charge leaves Sharpness South (formerly Oldminster) Junction after re-railing G.W. 0–4–2T No 1472. This was on 16.10.64 a fortnight before the withdrawal of the passenger service.

Berkeley Loop Junction signal box in May 1965 with Stinchcombe Hill in the background. The loop connecting the Berkeley Road–Sharpness branch with the main Gloucester–Bristol line has been lifted but it was regularly used for evening goods traffic between Lydney and Stoke Gifford before the accident involving the Severn Bridge. On some Sundays in winter when the Severn tunnel was closed for maintenance, passenger trains between Cardiff and Bristol also used this route. There was no road access to the junction.

G.W. 0-4-2T No 1472 returning light from Sharpness to Berkeley Road after being re-railed by the Gloucester breakdown train.

During 1964 condemned steam loco's were stored in the extensive sidings adjacent to Sharpness Docks. This picture shows a line of G.W.R. loco's waiting to be cut up. Date 16.10.64.

The bridge carrying the Severn & Wye Railway over the River Severn between Lydney and Sharpness was rendered useless when two spans were destroyed after 81 years of service. This scene from April 1964 shows the gap in the bridge and the remains of Severn Bridge Station. The stone arches just beyond the station spanned the Gloucester–South Wales main line.

The swing section of the Severn Bridge over the Sharpness–Gloucester canal in 1965. Power to operate the bridge was supplied by vertical boilered steam engines. it was opened in 1879 and closed at the end of October 1960 when oil tankers collided with the bridge after missing the entrance to the docks in fog and at night.

The rare and pleasing sight of a re-opened branch line. The L.M.S.R. once ran through passenger trains between Thornbury and Bristol, but the passenger service was withdrawn before the end of World War 2. Several years after the complete closure of the branch, British Rail re-opened the line from Yate to Tytherington and in this picture taken in 1982 a pair of class 37's can be seen at the quarries with a block stone train.

A G.W. "Hall" class 4-6-0 on the G.W. route from Bristol via Filton Junction, has diverged from the South Wales–Paddington mainline at Westerleigh West Junction and is heading north to join the M.R. Bristol–Gloucester route via Yate South flyover (since removed). In the background is the trackbed of the former spur for traffic heading east from Yate South. Date 14.8.65.

Mangotsfield station, closed since 1969, was at the western tip of a triangle. This photograph taken in April 1982 shows the canopy removed but platforms still intact. The trackbed of the Bristol–Gloucester main line is in the foreground and the platforms for the Bristol–Bath suburban services (withdrawn 1966) on the right. Before September 1962 the "Pines Express" took the third side of the triangle on the Bath–Gloucester section of its run between Bournemouth and Manchester.

At Bristol Temple Meads on Saturday 1.9.62. L.M.S. class 2 2–6–2T No 41296 is leaving on the 4.52 p.m. all stations to Bath Green Park via Mangotsfield. The recently arrived 11.35 a.m. Newquay–York has changed from diesel to steam haulage and L.M.S. "Jubilee" class 4–6–0 No 45675 "Hardy" will continue north calling at Mangotsfield and Gloucester Eastgate. Both trains take the M.R. route from Temple Meads which was closed completely to passenger traffic by 1970.

On the outskirts of Bath, L.M.S. class 2P 4-4-0 No 40569 and B.R. class 9 2-10-0 No 92203 head a Bournemouth–West Midlands train downhill between Coombe Down and Devonshire tunnels. After reversal at Bath Green Park, Gloucester Eastgate will be the next stop. This route, intensively used on Saturdays in Summer, no longer exists south of Westerleigh. 92203 is now preserved and named "Black Prince". Date 10.9.60.

Bristol Old Station and signal box on 7.9.63. About to draw forward from under Brunel's hammerbeam (decorative only) roof is the 5.15 p.m. stopping train to Birmingham via Gloucester and Worcester, hauled by L.M.S. class 5 4-6-0 No 44825.

Netherhope Halt, from the tunnel on the Wye Valley line leading to Tintern Quarry.

G.W. 0-6-0PT No 4671 descending from Tintern Quarry with a load of ballast shortly after passing the site of Tidenham Halt on 11.3.65. The Gloucester–South Wales line is in the foreground.

Wye Valley Junction, from the road bridge above the site of Tutshill Halt. A Newport–Gloucester D.M.U. meets G.W. 0-6-0PT No 4621 with a southbound pick up goods. The empty hopper wagons are probably bound for Tintern Quarry, up the branch climbing away on the left of the picture. Date 11.3.65.

Lydney station on 13.4.62 with G.W. 2-6-0 No 6330 on the 7.10 a.m. Gloucester–Newport. The line formerly leading to the docks crossed the main line at right angles on the left of the picture.

Lydney shed on 13.4.62 with G.W. 0-6-0PT's Nos 1632 and 4614 and two tender loco's facing the mainline and Gloucester.

Tufts Junction between Whitecroft and Lydney on 20.12.63. G.W. 0-6-0PT No 1631 is about to propel empties up the Oakwood branch to Princess Royal Colliery – workings visible in background.

G.W. 0-6-0PT No 1627 returning from Speech House Road to Coleford Junction on 1.2.61, viewed from a point between the two Cannop Ponds.

At Speech House Road on 1.2.61 G.W. 0-6-0PT No 1627 propels vans up the branch to the wood distillation plant.

G.W. 0-6-0PT No 1605 at Speech House Road on 27.10. 61.

A Stephenson Locomotive Society Special climbing to Serridge Junction from Speech House Road on 13.5.61. The loco's are G.W. 0-6-0PT's No 6437 (auto-fitted) and 8701 (pushing). This was the Severn & Wye route to Lydbrook Junction (after reversal at Serridge) and Cinderford.

Replenishing the tanks of 1631 at Parkend on a frosty morning in December 1963.

Two G.W. 0-6-0PT's make comparatively light work of the 1 in 31 Coleford branch on 14.1.65.

Birch twigs glisten in winter sunshine at the site of Point Quarry sidings as G.W. 0–6–0PT's Nos 8745 and 9711 return from Whitecliff Quarry to Coleford Junction. Date 14.1.65.

Coleford Junction on 14.1.65.

A Coleford branch gradient post.

The Coleford branch was not only very steep, but twisting. Here G.W. 0-6-0PT No 1631 negotiates a sharp curve hewn from the rock on the 1 in 30 descent to Coleford Junction. Date 1.2.61.

G.W. 0-6-0PT No 8701 descending from Coleford past Point Quarry. On the left, the earlier tramway route can be seen approaching and passing under the railway. Date 26.4.62.

The Severn & Wye station at Coleford on 2.7.64 with G.W. 0-6-0PT No 3737 shunting.

The G.W. station at Coleford on 1.2.61 with G.W. 0-6-0PT No 1631 about to leave for Whitecliff Quarry.

G.W. 0-6-0PT No 1631 eases itself over the catch points at the approach to Whitecliff Quarry. 1.2.61.

G.W. 0-6-0PT No 8745 shunting at Whitecliff Quarry west of Coleford on 14.1.65. Before 1918 the line continued to Monmouth.

G.W. 4–6–0 No 6987 "Shervington Hall" passing the western end of the Severn Bridge with a freight from South Wales on 18.4.64. Both bridges seen in the picture have since been dismantled.

The Cinderford branch token exchange apparatus stands in readiness at Bullo Pill West in July 1965.

Looking down river from above Bullo Pill on 24.9.65. G.W. 0-6-0PT No 4698 runs parallel with the Gloucester–South Wales main line before turning west up the steep branch to Cinderford

G.W. 0-6-0PT No 3643 seems to have disturbed the pigeons as it blasts away from Bullo Pill up the Cinderford branch. The signal is interlocked with catch points leading to a sand drag. Date 14.7.65.

G.W. 0–6–0PT No 1642 bursts out of Haie Hill tunnel and past Lower Soudley ground frame, with empties for Northern United Colliery. Date 27.10.61.

Interior of ground frame at Lower Soudley in 1965.

G.W. 0-6-0PT No 8729 climbing between Haie Hill and Bradley Hill tunnels on 13.4.62.

On 13.6.62 the Gloucestershire Railway Society ran a special train to Cinderford and up the Churchway branch; it is seen here propelled by G.W. 0-6-0PT No 6424, returning to Bullo Pill past Upper Soudley. A short, gated siding is hidden by the road in the foreground and behind the train is Bradley Hill tunnel.

After a short stop at Upper Soudley Halt to raise steam, G.W. 0-6-0PT No 1642 continues on its way up to Bilson Junction and Northern United Colliery. Date 27.10.61.

Amidst the dense foliage of high summer G.W. 0-6-0PT No 3665 emerges from Blue Rock tunnel with a train for Cinderford. Date 22.7.65.

With tank wagon brakes pinned down G.W. 2-6-2T No 4564 eases its load past Shake-mantle on the descent to Bullo Pill. Date 28.8.64.

G.W. 0-6-0PT No 8729 passes under the Cinderford–Blakeney road on 13.4.62. The disused sidings at Eastern United Colliery are on the left.

On 9.3.64 G.W. 0-6-0PT No 4698 passes the site of Staple Edge Halt. On the right are the derelict buildings of Eastern United Colliery, closed in 1959.

Ruspidge Halt (formerly Cinderford station) on the Cinderford–Coleford road, with G.W. 0-6-0PT No 4624 at the head of Northern United empties. Date 9.3.64.

G.W. 0-6-0PT No 3755 at Bilson Junction, Cinderford on 22.7.65. On the embankment to the north, the start of the semi-circular route to Cinderford station can be seen. Beyond, also on an embankment, running from left to right, is the Severn & Wye Railway connection to Cinderford. The Whimsey branch curves to the right and passes through a gap in the Severn & Wye embankment. Continuing straight ahead is the Churchway branch leading to Northern United Colliery.

G.W. 0-6-0PT No 4689 starts off up the Whimsey branch past an ancient wooden fixed distant for Bilson Junction. At one time this line extended beyond Drybrook to Mitcheldean Road. Date 19.8.65.

On 29.3.65 at Northern United Colliery G.W. 0-6-0PT No 4698 has propelled empties up from Bilson Junction and is running back to the brickworks junction to pick up loaded wagons visible on the right.

The Hereford branch platforms at Grange Court Junction on 25.10.64 a week before the passenger service was withdrawn. B.R. class 5 4-6-0 No 73021 is arriving from Hereford and one of Hereford's pannier tanks, No 4623, is about to return on the local pick up goods.

On 15.5.64 G.W. 4-6-0 No 7801 "Anthony Manor" climbs into the hills from Blaisdon with the 9.48 a.m. Gloucester–Hereford.

Oil lamps at Blaisdon Halt.

Longhope signal box.

G.W. 0-6-0 No 2241 pulls away from Longhope with the midday Gloucester–Hereford train. Date 20.11.63.

One of the more memorable sights on the single line from Grange Court Junction to Rotherwas Junction, Hereford, were the West of England–Liverpool expresses, diverted on winter Sundays from their normal route when the Severn Tunnel was closed for maintenance work. Here, the 8.40 a.m. from Plymouth, hauled by grimy G.W. 2-6-0's Nos 6319 and 7338, is approaching the rather overgrown eastern entrance to Lea Line Tunnel. Date 18.3.62.

A Hereford–Gloucester passenger hauled by G.W. 2-6-0 No 7319 leaving the eastern entrance to Lea Line tunnel on 22.6.64.

G.W. 4-6-0 No 7801 "Anthony Manor" leaving Lea Line tunnel with the 9.50 a.m. Gloucester–Hereford on 14.4.64.

G.W. 2-6-0 No 6349 leaving Mitcheldean Road with a train for Gloucester on 15.5.64.

Mitcheldean Road station on 14.4.64 with G.W. 0-6-0PT No 3728 leaving for Ross on Wye. The line to Drybrook and Cinderford (dismantled during World War One) left the station yard in the same direction before climbing steeply away to the south-west.

A G.W.R. "Manor" class 4-6-0 climbs through the cutting at the approaches to Mitcheldean Road station with a train from Hereford on 7.8.64. It was at this point that a stop board proclaimed "All down goods and mineral trains must STOP DEAD here" – for the purpose of pinning down wagon breaks.

G.W. 0–6–0 No 2273 in Ross on Wye engine shed on 3.3.62.

G.W. 0–6–0PT No 3728 draws its train away from the goods shed through Ross on Wye station to take water at the 'up' platform in readiness for a trip to Lydbrook. Date 14.4.64.

On 14.11.63 G.W. 0–6–0 No 2286 takes water at the east end of Ross on Wye station prior to working the Lydbrook line, seen branching to the right of the engine shed.

G.W. 0-6-0 No 2287 alongside the River Wye at Kerne Bridge with the afternoon Ross on Wye–Lydbrook goods. Date 2.7.64.

G.W. 0-6-0PT No 9665 crossing the River Wye with the Lydbrook goods shortly after passing Kerne Bridge station. Goodrich Castle is on the skyline. Date 10.3.61.

G.W. 0-6-0PT No 9711 leaving Lydbrook Junction for Ross on Wye on 30.3.65.

G.W. 0-6-0PT No 3728 at Lydbrook shortly after arrival from Ross on Wye on 14.4.64. In the foreground is the platform formerly served by the Severn & Wye line from Lydney via Serridge Junction.

Lydbrook Viaduct which carried the Severn & Wye Railway's connection between Lydbrook and Serridge Junctions.

An evening train from Hereford pulls away from Backney Halt on 22.6.64.

G.W. 4–6–0 No 7805 "Bradley Manor" crossing the River Wye between Backney and Fawley on the evening of 9.7.64 with a Hereford bound train.

The view from the South Wales road at Over near Gloucester. G.W. 0-6-0 No 2245 with the goods from Dymock, is about to join the South Wales–Gloucester mainline at Over Junction. Date 28.9.61.

On 23.6.62 a Gloucestershire Railway Society special starts off down the branch from Over Junction to Dymock with G.W. 0-6-0PT No 6424 in charge. Passenger services between Gloucester, Dymock and Ledbury were withdrawn three years before this date.

Between the B4215 road and the floodwaters of the River Leadon at Rudford, G.W. 0-6-0 No 2232 trundles its single wagon load towards Newent. Date 24.1.62.

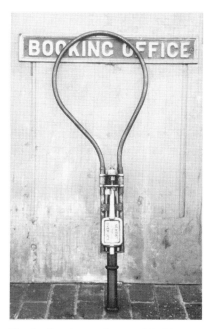

Single line key token and holder.

Newent station nears the end of its life on 7.12.63 as G.W. 2-6-2T No 5518 approaches from Dymock with the thrice weekly goods returning to Docks Branch Sidings, Over.

Ledbury station on 9.6.59. G.W. 2–6–2T No 4573 has run round its train, taken water at the platform end and is about to couple up for the 5.25 p.m. departure to Gloucester. A month after the photograph was taken the service was withdrawn.

For several years in the 1970's steam specials were allowed to operate between Didcot, Worcester and Hereford. In this scene a G.W.R. Society Special drifts downhill towards Ledbury from Colwall Tunnel in the Malvern Hills. Herefordshire Beacon is in the background.

"Sir Edward Elgar" nameplate.

The long way round for a Lydney Town–Sharpness school train. On 6.10.61 nearly a year after two spans of the Severn Railway Bridge were brought down, G.W. 0-6-0PT No 8717 crosses the River Severn at Over Junction, Gloucester, on a trip of nearly forty miles, with a quick water stop at Gloucester Central. Immediately beyond the bridge is the junction for Dymock.

Iron ore empties returning from South Wales to Banbury via Stratford and Fenny Compton, crossing the River Severn at Over Junction, Gloucester, behind B.R. class 9 2-10-0 No 92220 "Evening Star" on 2.10.61.

Condemned loco's await their fate on Gloucester Docks Branch sidings. Curving away to the left is the Castle Meads power station branch. In the foreground are "Castle" class "Earl of Plymouth" and pannier tank No 8701. Date 29.5.64.

On 14.12.63 Hymek No D7091 and L.M.S. "Jubilee" class 4–6–0 No 45690 "Leander" wait at the north end of Gloucester Central station. "Leander" was one of three "Jubilees" remaining from Bristol Barrow Road's previous (1961) allocation of nine.

Gloucester Central on 20.11.63. A Hymek is about to leave for Swindon with a three coach train recently arrived from Cheltenham behind G.W. 2–6–2T No 4564.

Redundant G.W. 0–4–2T's Nos 1420, 1472, 1458 and 1453 stand in front of Horton Road shed coaling stage shortly after the withdrawal of the Gloucester–Chalford service at the end of October 1964. The only survivors in this photograph, taken from the end of Eastgate station 'down' platform, are No 1420 and the wooden structure of the Mileage Yard Ground Frame.

On 19.9.64 G.W. 2–8–0 No 3812 heads west past Horton Road shed with a freight, including S.R. class M7 0–4–4T No 30111.

The busy level crossing at Tramway Junction on 14.10.65 with B.R. class 9 2-10-0 No 92227 heading north towards Cheltenham.

A string of light engines returning north, lay a smoke screen between Elmbridge and Churchdown. Date 28.11.65.

G.W. 4-6-0 No 7808 "Cookham Manor" passing Churchdown with the 1700 Gloucester Central–Cheltenham St. James on 4.10.65 less than three months before the end of steam traction on the Western Region of British Rail.

The 8.30 a.m. Cardiff–Newcastle passing Churchdown on 22.8.59 with L.M.S. class 4P compound 4-4-0 No 41123 piloting B.R. Caprotti class 5 4-6-0 No 73142. 41123 was the last of the once numerous class of 'Compounds' at work on the Bristol–Birmingham route.

On 18.2.62 L.M.S. "Jubilee" class 4–6–0 No 45568 "Western Australia" passes Church-down with the 8.40 a.m. Cardiff–Newcastle.

L.M.S. class 8F 2–8–0 No 48183 toils northward through Churchdown with a train of coal empties on New Year's Day 1962.